ENCHANTING
PENANG

DAVID BOWDEN

JOHN BEAUFOY PUBLISHING

Contents

Above left: Trishaws still transport people around historic George Town.

Above centre: Penang National Park is one the island's most serene places to visit.

Above right: Penang is home to hundreds of butterfly species including the Rajah Brooke's Birdwing.

Opposite: Witty street art by Lithuanian artist, Ernest Zacharevic.

Title page: The ornate entrance doors to Tua Pek Kong Temple, Tanjung Tokong.

Chapter 1: A Living Museum

Penang Island is rich in living history and full of vitality. While there are beaches along Batu Ferringhi on the north coast, it is George Town's history and culture that make this former spice island so unique and vibrant as a tourist destination.

George Town's narrow streets and historic buildings are the region's most intact assemblage of pre-war buildings, recognized in 2008 and protected by UNESCO as a World Heritage Site (a joint site with Melaka). Tourism has blossomed from this recognition, enhanced by an innovative street art programme as well as enlightened cultural festivals and events.

Penang, the state, includes the island and a stretch of land on the mainland centred on Butterworth. They are connected by two long and impressive road bridges. Penang's strategic location has meant that it has been a port of call for centuries for traders and travellers. First sailing ships, then steamers once called here and now cruise liners bring in the tourists. Penang International Airport is a hub

for northern Malaysia and the island's quality of life makes it a popular place for retirees.

In the 15th and 16th centuries, spices grown on Penang, such as pepper, cloves, nutmeg and mace, were eagerly sought by European nations. Nutmeg and mace were particularly important (nutmeg is a seed and mace the fleshy outer layer) and while native to just nine Indonesian islands in the Banda Sea, nutmeg trees (*Myristica fragrans*) thrived in tropical Penang.

The British first became interested in Penang later when much of Asia was still seen as a source of spices and other exotic commodities, such as tea from China. In the late 18th century, Captain Francis Light (his son, William surveyed and

laid out Adelaide, the South Australian capital), an officer with the Calcutta-based East India Company, proposed Penang as a commercial centre which he thought could outstrip Malacca (now spelt Melaka) in the south of the Malay Peninsula and become a convenient port to support the Chinese tea trade. Opium was traded in the reverse direction under British control from India to China via Penang. At one stage, tax on the shipment of opium into Penang was the largest contributor to the Government's coffers.

Light argued that Penang was a favourable location because ships could easily stop here plus there was an abundance of timber and vessels could re-supply with cargoes of tin, pepper, betel nut, rattan and birds' nests from the island and the mainland hinterland. He envisaged that Penang would develop into a significant regional trading hub and he was correct, as it quickly eclipsed Malacca due mainly to its free-trade status.

Left: Nutmeg and mace were the prized spices Europeans sought from Asia.

Above: An intricately decorated ceramic lintel in George Town.

Opposite: Terraces of old shophouses line many streets in historic George Town.

Geography and Climate

Opposite: Both George Town (foreground) and the mainland (background) are visible from Penang Hill.

Below left: One of the two bridges across the Straits of Malacca linking Penang to the mainland.

Penang is an island just off the mainland in north-western Peninsular Malaysia located between 100° 8' E and 100° 32' E longitude and 5° 8' N and 5° 35' N latitude. A 3-km (2-mile) stretch of the Straits of Malacca separates the island from the mainland on the east and the neighbouring Indonesian island of Sumatra on the west. The straits are one of the world's busiest waterways. Thailand is 150 km (93 miles) to the north.

There are, in fact, two Penangs; one is the island, the other, the state. The state is dominated by the island but a small strip of land on the mainland called Seberang Prai (formerly Province Wellesley) is also part of Penang State. They are connected by two bridges. At 1,048 km² (405 sq miles), Penang is Malaysia's second smallest state but it is larger than neighbouring islands, such as Langkawi, Phuket (Thailand) and Singapore.

While a densely populated island, this concentration is mostly around the fringes with the eastern and northern parts being the most urbanized. Development is limited in the centre with forests covering much of Penang Hill although development is encroaching upon the slopes. The lowlands of Penang's western and southern coastlines are sparsely settled and dominated by Penang National Park, mangrove forests and villages.

Being located just north of the Equator, Penang has an equatorial climate of year-round hot and humid conditions. Relief and rain arrive with the monsoon; the seasonal reversal of the winds once so important for sailing vessels crossing the oceans. It rains more heavily in Penang during the south-west monsoon from May to September.

Despite being only 823 m (2,750 ft) above sea level, the temperature on Penang Hill (Bukit Bendera) is noticeably cooler than the lowland and temperate pine trees flourish here. It was the cooler temperature that saw the establishment of Malaysia's first hill station. Heat-weary colonialists sought

refuge here as early as 1810 and Hotel Bellevue still accommodates those looking for a cool location.

While air-conditioning and fan-cooling are the norm in Penang, some buildings have incorporated features designed to reduce the heat. In old buildings, shuttered windows and large bamboo blinds keep out direct sunlight and traditional village homes are built on stilts to allow the air to circulate.

Another prominent architectural feature is the "five-foot way" which was introduced as a formal building by-law in Malaya in 1884. While normally private property, this covered and cool thoroughfare at the front of buildings was used by the public as a shaded footpath. They are still a feature of George Town and used by shopkeepers as a location on which to sell merchandise.

History

Penang's history is intricately linked to that of the East India Company (EIC) which was a chartered syndicate of traders operating under a loose British royal monopoly. It was established in 1591 by aristocrats and wealthy merchants to expedite trade with the East Indies and received a royal charter from Queen Elizabeth I in 1600. Its operations suited the Government as there was no state investment involved but much to be gained from royalties and taxes. The EIC imported Asian spices in competition with the Dutch, the Portuguese and then the French. This trade required protection from naval vessels, settlements and forts.

Below left: Fort Cornwallis provided defence for the original settlement.

Below: This cannon in Fort Cornwallis originally belonged to the United East India Company of Holland.

Opposite: The statue of Captain Francis Light at Fort Cornwallis.

The 17th to 19th centuries saw European expansion in the region and the era is typified by the Seri Rambai Cannon located in Fort Cornwallis. The letters "VOC" on it refer to the Verenigde Oostindische Compagnie (United East India Company) which vied with the EIC for regional domination. In 1606 this brass cannon was presented to the Sultan of Johor and then taken to Java by the Portuguese in 1613 where it stayed until 1795. It then went via Acheh to Selangor before being seized by the British and put in Fort Cornwallis in 1871. By the mid 18th century the East India Company controlled 72,500 tonnes (80,000 tons) of shipping crewed by 7,000 sailors and an army of 70,000 Indian soldiers.

A settlement was established on Penang in 1786 through the buccaneering efforts of Francis Light. Light was the last of a long line of EIC merchant adventurers and once he passed away, he was replaced by a new breed of civil service functionaries. Light successfully negotiated the leasing of Penang from Sultan Abdullah Makram Shah of Kedah as a trading base, in return for the promise – unfulfilled – of protection from external and internal threats.

Light saw the development of Penang with a commercial twinkle in his eye, overtly, though, he argued with the Company that it would offer a strategic base to counter the naval threat presented by the Dutch and French. In this new settlement, Francis Light saw the opportunity for personal wealth and advancement, and through its rapid growth, he was not disappointed.

By 1786, Sultan Abdullah discovered that the British wouldn't support him militarily against his northern Siam (present-day Thailand) foes. Tension surfaced in 1791 with Light fighting and defeating the Sultan's forces who were mounting an attack against him. In 1800 the British negotiated a land acquisition on the mainland, named Province Wellesley, in return for providing maritime security to Kedah and increasing the annual bounty paid to the Sultan.

Light died in Penang in 1794 aged 54 and was buried in the Protestant Cemetery on Jalan Sultan Ahmad Shah, George Town. A statue of Francis Light was erected at the entrance to Fort Cornwallis. It is possible to visit the former estate of Francis Light located on Jalan Ayer Itam close to the centre of George Town. Here Light established a simple wooden and *attap*-roofed home where he lived with his Eurasian wife Martina Rozells. The more substantive Anglo-Indian Georgian mansion called Suffolk House, which now stands here, was built after Light's death by William Phillips,

who later became the Governor. This became in turn Government House, the Governor's Residence, a school and the Japanese administrative centre during the Second World War, then finally fell into disrepair. It was restored and is now administered by Badan Warisan (Malaysia's National Trust). It is open for visits or for a meal in the stately restaurant.

Not long after Light raised the Union Jack in Penang in the name of King George III and named it Princes of Wales Island, Fort Cornwallis was built on the most easterly point of the coast. There had been a basic fort here which was reconstructed by convict labour from stone and brick in 1793. Not much of the fort now remains but its commanding harbourside location makes it a popular tourist attraction.

Initially, George Town's public facilities were limited and primitive but eventually a street grid was laid out and amenities provided. The first buildings were constructed from timber and thatching (*attap*) but eventually more permanent buildings replaced them. George Town's

Right: The stately Suffolk House stands on land originally farmed by Captain Francis Light. It has been restored and is worth visiting if only to dine in its grand restaurant.

Opposite top: Many old Chinese shophouses have been restored in Penang. Typically the ground floor operated as a shop while the family lived upstairs.

Opposite below: Penang's State Legislature Building, constructed in an Anglo-Indian classical style, dates back the 19th century.

Lloyd dominated shipping from Penang. Both nations established shipping facilities and one of the most interesting heritage walking trails in George Town is the German Trail.

While George Town's architectural styles are eclectic, the Chinese shophouse dominates. Designed by immigrant Chinese masterbuilders from Guangdong, these two or three-storey structures have a narrow street frontage and spacious interior airwells for light and ventilation. They were usually built from brick in terraces with uniform but often ornate façades. Similar buildings are found in Melaka and Singapore. Construction reached its peak in the 1920s during the rubber boom.

Penang is strategically located along the Straits of Malacca and over the centuries various embattlements have been built to protect it. Despite its fortifications, the British forces based at Bukit Batu Maung in the south-east of Penang's were unable to stop the Japanese invasion during the Second World War.

In 1957, the British colony of Malaya became the independent nation of Malaysia of which Penang was one of the states in the federation. Unlike some other states it has no Sultan but rather a Governor who is appointed by the constitutional King. Penang's Government is democratically elected with the Chief Minister heading the Dewan Undangan Negeri (State Legislative Assembly) whose building is on Light Street, George Town.

development was rapid and haphazard but emerged with a fort and a central *padang* (grassy field) as well as commercial and exclusive residential areas. This colonial zone radiating around the fort remains intact today.

Light created a free trading environment with cheap land and minimal governance and Penang continued as an entrepôt for many decades after his death. Trading houses, which all earned commission from dealing in valuable goods heading to Europe (it has been estimated that by the time spices arrived in Europe they were up to 60,000 times what they had been sold for in Asia), were established in George Town.

In 1826, Penang, Singapore and Malacca were administered by the British as the Straits Settlement. By the mid to late 19th century, steamships became important and the British P & O Company and Germany's Norddeutscher

The People

Today, Penang has a population of almost two million of whom approximately 60% live on the island and the remainder on the mainland. Demographers predict these figures will be reversed in years to come as the latter becomes more developed. Penang also has Malaysia's highest population density.

When Light arrived in Penang, the local Malay population was estimated to be just 136 villagers living in two coastal *kampungs* (villages). Numbers grew with the establishment of the British settlement due mostly to an influx of mainlanders escaping from the anarchy and lawlessness in Kedah during a conflict with neighbouring Siam.

Penang's original settlers were fishing folk and there are still some small villages and fishing communities scattered mostly around Penang's southern and western coasts. Boats tend to be small scale and sailed by just one or two crew, although there are some larger boats which head to sea for several days. One of the essential ingredients in many Malaysian dishes is *belacan* (fermented ground shrimp with salt) and there are several places on the west coast where the pungent mix is made by fisherfolk and dried on racks in the sun.

Penang advanced quickly from being a near-deserted island to one serving the maritime trade. It was established to support global trade and skilled workers arrived from the mainland, China, India, the Middle East and England. Penang began as and remains a very cosmopolitan island. In 1804, Sir George Leith, the Lieutenant-Governor said: "There is not, probably, any part of the world where, in so small a space so many different people are assembled together, or so great a variety of languages spoken." According to the last census in 2010, 45.6% of Penang residents are Chinese, 43.6% Bumipatra (Malays and others), 10.4% Indian and 0.4% others.

The Malaysian population is a young one with 27% of the people below 15 years of age. A near traditional lifestyle is not unusual for many young people who live away from Penang's urban areas. On the western and southern coasts many children live in *kampungs* or villages, playing in semi-rural surroundings and learning to fish.

The Chinese mainly came from coastal regions like Canton (Guangzhou) and Hokkiens from Fujian. In the early 19th century, the Hakka people from southern China started to arrive. They were supported by the various *kongsi* societies that evolved to assist their fellow countrymen. While not as significant as in Malacca, some Chinese intermarried with local Malays thus creating the Baba Nonya or Peranakan culture (Baba being males of the intermarriage and Nonya the women).

Penang's Indian community is as complex as that of the Chinese. Many came as convicts to build public infrastructure, while others came as free settlers and some arrived as indentured labour for a set period on a fixed wage. Some of the convicts remained after completing their sentence. Indian troops accompanied Light when he established the settlement, many of whom were Bengali and Tamil Moslems, who subsequently established Penang's famous Kapitan Keling Mosque. Another group of Indian migrants was the Chettiar of Tamil Hindu descent, who became prominent

investors, spice traders and money lenders.

Penang's cultural melting pot is what makes it so fascinating. Different languages are spoken, foods eaten, religions observed, festivals celebrated, clothes worn and buildings erected. Many streets in George Town reflect this with the range of hawker foods being one of the most obvious signs.

Left: Some children on the south coast live in villages and fish along the muddy foreshore.

Above: Hindus visit temples and smash coconuts during the Thaipusam festival.

Opposite: Fisherfolk dry shrimp paste on racks in the sun.

Religion

Penang is a multi-denominational island with the majority of its people being followers of Islam, Hinduism, Christianity, Buddhism or Taoism.

Penang's Muslim community has local roots as well as an input from migrants and travellers from distant shores. Masjid Terapung Tanjung Bungah (Tanjung Bungah Floating Mosque) on the northern beaches is arguably Penang's grandest mosque. Its seven-storey minaret towers over the coastline and its interior can accommodate 1,500 worshippers. While it is actually built on stilts, it gives the appearance of floating on the water and is Malaysia's first such mosque.

Hindu temples are found on both the island and the mainland. Sree Maha Mariamman Devasthanam Temple in Butterworth is typical of most with its brightly coloured sculptures of Hindu goddesses, gods, soldiers, chariots and floral decorations.

The Church of the Immaculate Conception on Lorong Maktab was the first church to provide mass to Roman Catholics. St George's Church on Lebuh Farquhar was Penang's first Anglican church consecrated in 1819.

Chinese temples have evolved from humble shrines to ornate temples dedicated to Buddhist and Taoist deities typically with ornate and auspicious lintels and rooflines. Many are designed according to *feng shui* principles (a Chinese philosophical system of harmonizing human existence with the surrounding environment). Various temples line Armenian Street in George Town. Two of the most visible are the Yap and Chee Keong Temples near the Cannon Street corner.

Penang has many ornately decorated Taoist temples. After being relocated from nearby Southbay property development site, the recently built Teng (or Cheng) Chooi Keong Temple at Batu Maung near the airport is a colourful structure that venerates Chor Soo Kong (the same deity as the nearby Snake Temple). Exquisite dragons bestride the roofline and others delicately carved into granite pillars stand guard at the entrance.

Shrines are evident in the homes of many Chinese Malaysians. A wall-mounted Kitchen God is a common feature at the entrance. This is a domestic god that protects the hearth and the family. Food and incense will often be offered to the god.

Above: Terapung Tanjung Bungah Mosque 'floats' on the northern coastline.

Right: Penang is also home to several Thai-styled Buddhist temples, such as Wat Chayamangkalaram.

Festivals

Festivals are an important part of Penang's cultural fabric and many are observed with a holiday. Its multiculturalism and religious diversity ensure that visitors have many opportunities to see some unique festivals. Celebrations include Chinese New Year, Chingay, Chap Goh Mei, Hungry Ghost Festival, Wesak, Thaipusam and Christmas Day.

Right: Raucous and acrobatic lion dances are commonly performed during Chinese New Year.

Opposite: The three-day Hindu festival of Thaipusam attracts a huge crowd in Penang with most climbing the 500 steep steps to pray at the Arulmigu Balathandayuthapani Temple.

Many Penang streets are decorated with red lanterns during the Chinese New Year whose dates vary but is usually celebrated in late January or early February. The Chinese celebrate with fireworks, family reunions and an extended holiday when many businesses close for at least a week. Lion and dragon dances bring good fortune. Skilful lion movements are accompanied by synchronized and loud sounds created by drums, cymbals and gongs. Chingay is a street parade celebrated during Chinese New Year where performers balance giant flagpoles on various parts of their body. The end of the celebrations are signified by Chap Goh Mei, when the women of Penang throw mandarins in the sea in search of a partner. The Hungry Ghost Festival is a month long festival spanning August and September when the Chinese pay homage to their ancestors.

Many Chinese people in Penang are Buddhists and observe the holiday and festival of Wesak. This is an auspicious day to celebrate the birth, enlightenment and passing of Lord Buddha. Most Buddhists light candles and pray at temples, such as the Reclining Buddha (Wat Chayamangkalaram), or join the float procession that follows a 7-km (4⅓-mile) long route through George Town.

Thaipusam is a colourful Hindu festival and holiday celebrated on the full moon of the Tamil month of Thai in late January or early February by Tamil descendants. Celebrated over three days, some devotees carry *kavadis* (weighted objects) to burden themselves as they ask for help or forgiveness from Lord Murugan. Some pierce their skin to show the extent of their austerity while others fast, pray, shave their heads and participate in a pilgrimage to Arulmigu Balathandayuthapani Temple 500 steps above Waterfall Road near the Botanic Gardens. The festival starts with a chariot procession that weaves from George Town to Waterfall Road. Hindus visit and pray at several temples and smash coconuts to symbolize the shattering of the ego in the pursuit of self-realization. A carnival atmosphere is created by stalls distributing food and selling bright decorations, accompanied by loud music. Thaipusam ends on day three when the chariot returns to George Town.

There are some fascinating cultural events such as the Penang Island Jazz Festival staged in late November or early December at a resort located beside the refreshingly cool Batu Ferringhi beachfront. The line-up includes international artistes and Malaysia's best jazz musicians.

Cuisine

When the *New York Times* and *Lonely Planet* acknowledged the street food of Penang as one of the world's finest travel experiences, they confirmed what the locals had known for years. Travellers come in their droves to eat and the locals realise the benefits of Penang's enticing and affordable street food.

Penang's multiculturalism ensures that the best Malay, Indian, Chinese and Peranakan food as well as a growing menu of creditable Western styles are plentiful. Street and hawker food reigns supreme and Malaysians travel here to sample the many famous dishes and popular hawkerstalls. Iconic *kopitiam* (coffeeshops) and cafés seem to open on a daily basis and now some very innovative food and wines from around the globe are also on offer.

Hawkerstalls

Malaysians consider Penang a paradise for hawker food. It is served all over Penang, mostly around the clock. In the old days, hawkers used to wander the streets selling their food from cane baskets carried over their shoulders. Some vendors still operate on the street but many offer this "meals on wheels" service from the back of motorbikes.

Penangites have their favourite hawkerstalls but those in the open air along Gurney Drive consistently rank near the top. Speciality stalls sell prawn *lam mee* (yellow rice noodles in prawn gravy), *sotong bakar* (grilled squid), Penang *laksa* (curry noodles), *ais kacang* (shaved ice with sweet delights) and *burbur cha cha* (coconut milk with sweet potato). *Satay* is also a speciality. While various Asian countries argue over the origins of *satay*, few deny its universal appeal. Small morsels of marinated meat (chicken or beef) are marinated for hours in spice powders of turmeric, coriander and lemongrass plus shallots, then threaded onto bamboo sticks and barbecued over sizzling charcoal. Once cooked, *satay* sticks are served with onions, cucumber, a spicy peanut sauce and, occasionally, cubes of rice.

Penangites snack a lot and dishes are not overly big. Some stalls only open at certain times of the day when the dish is most popular and several stalls may be located in a coffeeshop. Others may be temporary stalls by the side of the road with a few plastic chairs for patrons.

Opposite top: *Beef and chicken 'satay' are usually sold by the stick with half a dozen or a dozen being common quantities to order.*

Opposite below: *The smell of barbecued 'satay' wafts through many food courts and hawker areas.*

Above: *Gurney Drive food stalls make up Penang's most famous congregation of outdoor eating places.*

Right: *Muslim women selecting 'halal' hawker food.*

and spring onions in a chicken broth). Sisters Fried Kway Teow is a now-famous dish that has been made by two sisters for over 55 years. They can be found in Lam Heng Café on Jalan Macalister.

Hainanese chicken rice, fried rice, *dim sum* (various small steamed or fried delicacies), Hokkien *mee* (wok-fried noodles) are other well known Chinese dishes. Seafood dishes, such as fried garoupa, buttered prawns and oyster omelette, are prepared Chinese-style in many restaurants.

Chinese food

Chinese food is especially popular. Many famous Penang Chinese dishes were introduced by the Hokkiens, including *char kway teow* (a complex, wok-fried dish with many ingredients including flat rice noodles, soy sauce, chilli, prawns, cockles, bean sprouts, egg and *belachan*) and *kway teow* soup (flat rice noodles, chicken, prawns, bean sprouts

Malay food

Most Malay food is spicy with chilli, onions, garlic, lemongrass, ginger and *belacan* being important ingredients in many dishes. Chicken, beef and seafood are invaluable sources of protein while rice is a staple. A feature of Malay food is that it is *halal* (pork-free and prepared according to Islamic laws) and alcohol is not served.

Indian and Mamak food

Indian and Mamak dishes (Indian-Muslim) are keenly sought-after in Penang, the most famous being *nasi kandar* (steamed rice accompanied by curries and other dishes). Penang is considered to have Malaysia's best and the locals will argue over the merits of various stalls. Once peddled around the streets with containers of food suspended over a *kandar* (pole), it is now sold in stalls and coffeeshops all over the island. Famous stalls include Kayu, Line Clear, Al-Hass, Nasi Beratur, Kassim Mustafa and Kapitans.

Another popular dish is *rojak* which simply means "mixed" and there are two main versions; one with fruit and one savoury. The savoury version includes bean curd, boiled potatoes, bean sprouts, prawn fritters, hard-boiled egg and cucumber with liberal lashings of a spicy peanut sauce. The fruit version varies but commonly includes pineapple, green apples and green mango.

Food from both North and South India is served in Penang. Spicy curries are the standard fare but with support from many other dishes, such as *nasi biryani* which is a rice dish prepared with spices and *ghee*. Many Indians are Hindu and therefore don't eat beef but chicken, vegetables and seafood are plentiful. Rice is popular in South Indian dishes, such as banana leaf curry (rice, vegetables and meat served on a leaf), while breads such as *naan* are more common in North Indian cuisine. Spicy *tandoori* chicken prepared in a clay oven, fish head curry and *thosai* (a rice and lentil flour pancake) are other Indian dishes to try.

Many locals eat *roti canai* or *roti jala*, especially for breakfast. Both are wheat flour-based breads but made very differently. *Roti canai* is an Indian-inspired, circular flat bread made with oil, margarine or ghee and kneaded, flattened and oiled before being twirled in the air much like an Italian pizza. It is then fried until it is soft and flaky. There are many variations from savoury to sweet with the former being mostly served with *dhal* or curries. *Roti telur* (with an egg) is the most common variation. *Roti jala* is made from a liquid batter poured onto a skillet from a container with holes in the base. The resultant lace-like bread is served with the same accompaniments as *roti canai*.

Indian snacks, such as *pakora*, *vadi* and *samosa*, are sold for eating between meals over a cup of tea or coffee.

Above left: Roti canai' is a popular breakfast comprising flour and ghee that is fried on a hot plate and served with dhal or curry sauce.

Opposite top: Fried rice is found all over Penang in various dishes including those with fried egg and chicken 'satay'.

Opposite bottom: Sweet Malay cakes or 'kuih' are sold as snacks.

Markets

Night markets or *pasar malam* are well patronized by locals in the late afternoon to early evening. Makeshift markets are established on different nights of the week around the island. Stallholders set up and usually offer one or a few dishes that they have prepared or cooked at home before adding the finishing touches in the market. Many people buy raw ingredients to cook at home or purchase ready-to-eat meals, with *satay* being a favourite.

Being an island, fresh seafood is served everywhere. Many shoppers buy fish, prawns and other seafood from local markets along with exotic fruits, such as pomegranate, lychee, durian and mangosteen, and unusual vegetables, like petai.

Nonya cuisine

Malaysians were possibly the first to experiment with fusion cuisine long before it became fashionable. When Chinese males (Baba) married local Malay wives (Nonya), Nonya or Peranakan cuisine followed. Over time, Chinese ingredients were blended with Malaysian spices to create the distinctive style. *Asam* fish, beef *rendang* and *laksa* are iconic dishes that use some of the classic ingredients of ginger, coconut milk, candlenuts, pandan leaves, *belacan*, tamarind and lemongrass.

A famous Penang Nonya dish is *asam laksa* known for its sour flavour. Short rice noodles form the basis of the dish to which a spicy, fish-based broth flavoured with ginger flower, *belacan*, chilli, turmeric and lemongrass is added. Tamarind provides a degree of tartness. The dish is served in a bowl and topped with grated cucumber, pineapple, onions, ginger flower, mint and chillies.

Other tasty morsels include *cempedak* which is a very large strong smelling fruit related to a jackfruit. On the tree, the outside is green but inside it's full of sweet yellow pods containing a seed. The flesh can be eaten raw or battered, fried and served hot.

The restaurant scene

Smart cafés and restaurants plus some quirky bars have opened in recent years in line with the general growth in tourism in historic George Town. These serve local favourites as well as international comfort dishes to hungry and thirsty global travellers. One of the liveliest places to visit from breakfast to late is ChinaHouse. It offers something for every dining moment of the day. ChinaHouse is an impressive heritage development of cafés, bars, art spaces, retail and music venues covering three old shoplots. Restaurant Suffolk House is the venue for a grand meal in heritage surroundings.

In Penang culture, drinks are an important part of any meal, as is the coffeeshop or *kopitiam*. Malaysian coffeeshops are not coffeeshops in the European sense although coffee is served (*kopi* translates as coffee) but it isn't the only item on offer; they also serve tea (*teh*) and other hot and cold beverages. Beer may be sold in Chinese and Indian coffeeshops but never in a Malay or Mamak-operated one. Often the owner will sell the beverages and a few food items but will lease out space to other food sellers. In really busy coffeeshops, some half a dozen vendors will sell food items but usually only one or two dishes each which they specialize in.

Roasting coffee beans (usually with margarine) was commonly practised but most coffeeshops buy in pre-roasted beans these days. Ordering in a coffeeshop can be a minefield as there are many variations on the theme. Condensed milk rather than fresh milk is used. *Teh tarik* (stretched tea) is the best known beverage and is made by passing tea from one container to another to create a frothy head.

The coffeeshop is also a place in which to relax over a drink, view international football matches and watch the world go by and therefore serves a valuable social function as a place to meet.

Opposite top: One of Penang's most famous hawker foods is the sour fish-based noodle broth called 'asam laksa'.

Opposite below: Seafood such as squid and cockles is an essential ingredient in many Penang dishes.

Below: The elegant dining room in Suffolk House.

Natural Habitats

In 1786 when Francis Light first raised the Union Jack over Penang, the island was covered in dense rainforest and was uninhabited apart from a handful of Malay fishing villages and Bugis pirates. While pockets of primary vegetation remain today, the island has been altered for urban, agricultural, tourism and industrial development. In general, the west, the south and the mountainous interior are the least developed.

There are six recognized natural habitats found on the island. These are lowland dipterocarp forest, hill dipterocarp forest, beach, peat swamp forest, mangroves and a very obscure and unique habitat called meromictic lake.

Penang National Park in the north-west of the island is one of two federally funded national parks in Malaysia (the other being Taman Negara). This is the best part of Penang to see examples of all of the natural habitats.

Lowland and Hill Dipterocarp Forests

Lowland dipterocarp forest is the most common rainforest in Malaysia. In Penang, stands of primary forest still exist mostly on the western side of the island. Some areas that resemble primary forest are actually secondary forests having once been logged. Rainforest soils are nutrient poor therefore mushrooms, such as bracket fungi, are essential as they are decomposers and recyclers of nutrients.

Hill dipterocarp forest is similar to that of the lowland but is distinguished by *Shorea curtisii* tree species. Hill dipterocarp forest is generally supported on land above 750 m (2,460 feet). While Penang Hill (Bukit Bendera) isn't high enough for montane forest to develop, temperate pine trees flourish here in the cooler conditions.

Both lowland and hill dipterocarp forests are stratified into five distinct layers with tall emergents penetrating the 45-m (148-ft) high canopy. Beneath the discontinuous canopy layer is the main storey that grows to a height of 30 m (98 ft). In undisturbed forests, it is difficult for sunlight to penetrate the two upper layers and the understorey and forest floor, making up the final two layers, are usually not very dense. Creepers, vines, climbers and epiphytes are commonly found in the lower storeys with many growing on larger plants.

Sandy Beach and Rocky Shore

Being an island, there are several areas lined with beaches. Many of these have been modified by human activity but the sandy beaches of Penang National Park are mostly untouched. Pantai Kerachut and Pantai Ketapang are two pristine beaches.

In destinations such as the national park, lowland forests meet the quartz-sand beaches which are fine enough to enable Green, Hawksbill and Olive-Ridley Turtles to lay their eggs in the sands just beyond the foreshore. The Department of Fisheries manages a turtle hatchery on Pantai Kerachut to ensure a greater survival rate of the turtle hatchlings.

Above: Sandy beaches are mostly found on the northern and north-western coastlines.

Opposite: Lush tropical rainforests once covered much of Penang and still flourish in Penang National Park.

Peat Swamp Forest

Peat swamp forests are typically low in nutrients so that plants, such as pitcher plants, survive here by obtaining food not from the soil but mostly from insects or fallen leaf litter. *Nepenthes ampullaria* is a pitcher plant that survives in Penang National Park where warm and moist conditions plus soils low in nutrients are conducive to its growth. Insects fall into the cup-shaped plant, then decompose to provide the necessary nutrients.

Mangroves

Excellent stands of mangroves line much of Penang's west coast as well as the riverbanks of the small fishing village of Kuala Sungai Pinang. Mangroves have adapted to survive in saline and brackish water and many species have pneumatophores – lateral roots which grow upward to enable the plant to obtain oxygen. Mangroves serve many important functions from being a source of timber to providing a valuable habitat for marine organisms, such as oysters, crabs and mudskippers, as well as waterbirds, reptiles and monkeys. They also protect the coastline from wave damage, storm surges and even tsunamis, as their extensive root system consolidates the mud.

Lakes

Penang's largest expanse of water is the manmade Teluk Bahang Dam in the far north-west of the island. The dam provides water for domestic use and the island's famous dragon boat races are contested here.

Penang National Park is home to a rather unusual habitat called a seasonal meromictic lake located at the back of Pantai Kerachut (Kerachut Beach). This type of lake has separate layers of fresh and salty water that only intermix just once a year. Apart from being a picturesque lake that has a narrow opening to the sea, it is of great interest to scientists as it's just one of three of its type in Asia. The lake's stratification creates radically different environments for organisms that survive here. It forms during the monsoon seasons but at other times it may not be evident.

Opposite top: Carnivorous pitcher plants survive in nutrient-poor soils.

Opposite below: Mangrove-lined streams thrive on Penang's west coast.

Above: The meromictic lake in Penang National Park.

Flora and Fauna

Despite being a densely populated and highly urbanized island, there are places to see an abundance of tropical flora and fauna. Birdwatchers will especially enjoy coastal stretches that waders frequent and even the landscaped gardens of large resorts where flowers attract different types of birds. The best locations for seeing the island's flora and fauna are Penang National Park, Botanic Gardens, Penang Hill and several smaller recreational forest reserves called Hutan Lipur. Hutan Lipur Teluk Bahang is located near Batu Ferringhi and has the added attraction of a forestry museum.

Below: While typically found in Penang's forests, it is not unusual to see primates like the Long-tailed Macaque on some of the island's beaches.

Animals and birds

Lizards, big and small, are commonly seen. The largest is the Water Monitor (*Varanus salvator*) which is the region's second largest lizard after the Komodo Dragon. Adults generally grow to 2 m (6²/₃ ft) but can be bigger and attain an adult weight of 19 kg (42 lb). They move quickly across the ground when threatened and are excellent swimmers especially around Penang's mangroves. They are carnivores and often eat road carrion.

One of the most commonly seen primates throughout Penang and Southeast Asia is the Long-tailed Macaque (*Macaca fascicularis*). Noted for its long tail, this monkey is also known as the Crab-eating Macaque, which may explain its not uncommon appearance along Penang's beaches and wetlands. They may be seen in troops of up to 30, often with half as many males as females. Females stay with one troop for life but adult males move between troops.

The Silvered-leaf Langur (*Trachypithecus cristatus*) is much more docile, rarely leaving its home in the middle canopy of the rainforest. Adults have a long tail and grey-tipped black fur that gives it a silver sheen. Juveniles have orange fur. Groups with one male adult range from ten to 40 in number.

Wader birds are commonly seen around the shallow waters lining Penang. Egrets and herons are the most apparent because they are relatively large birds but there are many other smaller species to be observed.

The Little Heron (*Butorides striata*) is a wader that can be spotted along the mudflats, shallow waters and mangroves lining parts of Penang. Kuala Sungai Pinang on the northwest of the island is the ideal destination to see the Little Heron and several other species.

The Little Egret (*Egretta garzetta*) is another commonly seen wader especially in the shallows of wetlands. This bird has an all-white plumage, long black legs and a slim black bill. It feeds in the shallows on amphibians, reptiles, fish, insects and crustaceans.

Another wader that inhabits similar locations is the Grey Heron (*Ardea cinerea*) which feeds on frogs, insects and fish that it spears with its long slender bill. It is a large bird standing 100 cm (39 in) tall and has grey plumage above and white plumage below. It has a yellow bill and flies with its long neck in a distinctive S-shape.

The White-breasted Sea Eagle (*Haliaeetus leucogaster*) soars high on the thermals over coastal Penang. It has a white head and belly, grey feathers on the upper parts and black under-wing flight feathers. It catches fish with its talons and makes a large stick nest high up in trees.

A bird that lives among the reedbeds is the Yellow Bittern (*Ixobrychus sinensis*). It is mostly observed flying as it is difficult to see within reedbeds where it is camouflaged. They are a resident bird of Penang and make their nests on a bed of reeds.

Above: White-breasted Sea Eagles are often sighted soaring high on thermals or close to the water's edge taking fish in their strong talons.

Below left: The Yellow Bittern is well camouflaged amongst the reedbeds where it lives and nests.

Below: The Little Egret, a small white heron, feeds in the shallows of wetlands.

Plants

Penang's endemic plants are a product of the tropical climate, although some temperate species thrive in the higher and cooler parts of Penang Hill.

Many visitors staying in the resorts of Batu Ferringhi will find they're surrounded by lush, landscaped gardens of tropical flowers, some of which will be native and others introduced. These include colourful frangipani, lilies and orchids.

Penang's tropical rainforests are some of the most species-rich of any forests in the world. The plant life is complex and varied with many different species of all sizes, shapes and colours.

One of the common features of Penang's forests is the presence of epiphytes; those plants that grow on other plants for support. The Oak Leaf Fern (*Drynaria quercifolia*) is a common species in open habitats of the lowland. Epiphytes aren't parasites as they only use their host for support while obtaining nutrients from rainwater and falling leaf litter. Half of Malaysia's 500 species of ferns are epiphytic.

Above: Fishtail Palms thrive in the Botanic Gardens.

Left: Many of the island's gardens support frangipani flowers.

Top: The Entopia by Penang Butterfly Farm and Botanic Gardens is one of the best places to see some of the 850 species of orchids that are found in Peninsular Malaysia.

The Fishtail Palm (*Caryota uren*) is found in Penang's lowland forest and is named after its fan-shaped leaflets that resemble a giant fishtail. There are 13 species native to the region and they prefer moist areas, especially the rainforest understorey, in places like the Botanic Gardens. Sap from the flowers is also used to make an alcoholic drink.

The Traveller's Palm (*Ravenala madagascariensis*) originates from the Indian Ocean island of Madagascar. It isn't a true palm but a member of the bird of paradise family that grows to 7 m (23 ft) and features distinctive paddle-shaped leaves. It is a common and striking ornamental plant found all over the island.

Above: The Bird's Nest Fern is a large species that traps falling leaves and vegetable matter.

Above right: The Traveller's Palm thrives in the Penang Botanic Gardens.

Right: Epiphytes use a host tree for support.

Arts and Crafts

Many of George Town's old buildings were once home to various trades that are now dying out. Visitors have to be observant to find Chinese signboard carvers, Nonya beaded shoemakers, rattan furniture weavers, joss-stick makers, *mahjong* tile makers, wooden clog makers, goldsmiths and printers, but they do exist. However, artisan skills and traditional crafts and trades as well as traditional performing arts are seeing a resurgence due mainly to tourism. George Town is the best place to find these craftspeople still at work in the front of their shops.

Below left: A new generation of jewellers, glass blowers, artists and photographers is slowly turning historic George Town into a heritage city for the arts and crafts.

One of Penang's most famous sons is Dato' Jimmy Choo, the London-based fashion designer best known for his *haute couture* footwear. He comes from a family of shoemakers and made his first shoe at just 11 years old. Makers of Nonya beaded shoes are still found in Penang ensuring the continuity of this time-consuming trade.

Rattan cane grows in Penang's rainforests and is used to make furniture. This spiky palm differs from other palms in having a vine-like stem. Once harvested into thin, slender strands, it can be woven into various shapes. Rattan is ideal as it is lightweight, durable, flexible and strong. Shops selling rattan baskets, chairs and decorative fittings still operate in Penang.

Batik is a type of textile in which patterns are created using wax to mask certain areas of the cloth. Repeated waxing of different areas and subsequent dyeing enables different parts of the cloth to be coloured. Motifs of leaves and flowers, and geometrical designs are popular in Malaysia. There are various types of *batik* including those that use wooden blocks to stamp a design or the more modern forms using a paint brush. Resorts and shops along Batu Ferringhi conduct *batik* making classes and sell readymade textiles.

Penang has several art galleries most of which are privately owned. ChinaHouse Penang (153-155 Beach

Street) covers three expansive shoplots and not only includes a restaurant, bar, wine cellar and courtyard café but also has two dedicated art spaces, a music venue and an area for theatre. This and other art galleries support local and international artists and photographers through exhibitions.

Penang Museum and Art Gallery houses state relics, photos and heritage maps plus other historical and cultural artefacts. Penang State Art Gallery in Dewan Sri Pinang houses a permanent collection by local artists as well as presenting visiting exhibitions.

In August (although the date can vary), the streets of George Town are the focus for the George Town Festival. This month-long cultural event features performances that interact with and inspire audiences while taking a fresh approach to traditional Southeast Asian arts and that use

historic George Town as a performance space. Limits aren't set by the organizers and can range from concert hall performances to those staged in George Town's heritage streets or back lanes. The festival showcases creative local talent as well as internationally acclaimed theatre, dance, opera, music and film.

Left: Performers at the George Town Festival use the city's historic spaces as a stage.

Above: Visitors can watch 'batik' being made or try designing their own souvenir cloth to take back home.

Sports and Lifestyles

Watersports, such as jet skiing and sailing, are available in the waters surrounding Penang. Parasailing is a must-try activity for visitors staying along Batu Ferringhi (see page 54). Dragon boat races are an ancient and competitive sport with their origins in China. The Penang International Dragon Boat Festival in June has been staged at Teluk Bahang Dam for decades. It attracts crews from around the world who contest races of 200 m (219 yards) and 500 m (547 yards) in length with crews of up to 22 members. The larger boats have 18-20 paddlers, one drummer and one navigator.

Horse races are held regularly at the Penang Turf Club. This is also Malaysia's oldest members' club, established in 1864, four years before Malaysia's second oldest, the Penang Club.

International sporting events include the Penang Bridge International Marathon in November and the Penang International Triathlon and Duathlon in March.

Because of the heat, indoor sports, such as badminton, squash, tennis and sepak takrow (foot volleyball using a rattan ball), are also popular. In fact, the current world number 1 women's squash player, Datuk Nicol David, hails from Penang.

Despite the heat and humidity, there are shaded roads and trails that are perfect for mountain biking. Some resorts hire out bicycles and once away from the traffic in resort areas like Batu Ferringhi, the road conditions are perfect.

ESCAPE Adventureplay is an adventure park located in forests just south of Teluk Bahang with ropes, ladders, slides and climbs to challenge and thrill adventure seekers of all ages in a safe environment. The Gecko Towers enable visitors to experience a climbing wall, Atan's Leap allows safe freefalling and Monkey Business is designed to hone balancing skills. Over time, the park will expand with a Waterplay section and Treetops Hotel.

Naturalists at The Habitat Penang Hill guide visitors along nature trails to explore the flora and fauna. You can also explore the rainforest on the 230-m (755-ft) long Langur Way Canopy Walk and visit Curtis Crest Tree Top Walk at the summit of Penang Hill for 360° views.

There are several popular golf courses in the state on both the island and the mainland. Penang Golf Club (formerly Bukit Jambul Country Club) in the south-east at Bayan Lepas is the island's premier course. This 18-hole championship course has a rolling topography in the Penang foothills and an adjoining resort hotel.

While the Batu Ferringhi beachfront is lined with Hobie and Top Cat operators, sailing is a developing sport in Penang. There is a marina, retail (including the Royal Selangor Pewter Visitors Centre) and entertainment complex at Straits Quay, Tanjung Tokong, which is used by some local sailors as well as international crews passing through the Straits of Malacca. In November, yachts in Malaysia's leading offshore race, the Raja Muda Selangor International Regatta, stop at Straits Quay on their journey from Klang to Langkawi.

Opposite: Teams from around the world compete in the Penang International Dragon Boat Festival.

Right: The Habitat Penang Hill provides an authentic, diverse and educational Malaysian rainforest experience.

Top: ESCAPE is a well-designed park that has many adventurous rope activities.

Chapter 2: Historic George Town

The most densely populated part of Penang Island is a narrow coastal strip stretching from George Town to Batu Ferringhi including places such as Gurney Drive, a road beside the sea that has become famous for its hawkerstalls. George Town, the historic centre, was named after George III, the King of England. It became the first Malaysian town to be granted city status in 1957; 15 years ahead of the capital Kuala Lumpur.

Above: George Town is a maze of streets, heritage buildings and narrow passageways where many fascinating events occurred over the years. Nowadays it attracts a new generation craving espresso coffees or glasses of Pinot Noir rather than the traditional artisans like goldsmiths, carvers and joss-stick makers. Many of the latter are sunset trades as the children of these artisans seek more lucrative livelihoods. Traditional shops are slowly being replaced by contemporary retailing but medical halls, such as Kee Sang Tong, provide an example of living history for which Penang is so famous.

George Town has the region's best preserved collection of pre-Second World War houses and shoplots. As Malaysia opened up so did trade and with the discovery of tin, ports like Penang became important. As goods were loaded and unloaded, commercial properties and warehouses developed especially along Beach Street (Lebuh Pantai) which, before reclamation, once formed the coastline. Many grand buildings along Beach Street include Ban Hin Lee Bank, George Town Dispensary, Kongsoon House, Sandilands Buttery, India House and British India House.

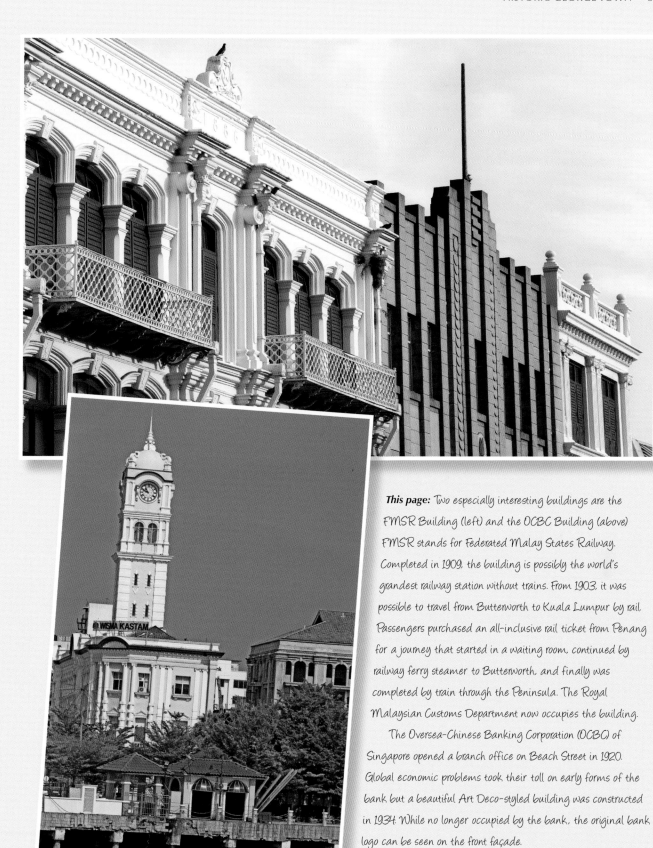

This page: Two especially interesting buildings are the FMSR Building (left) and the OCBC Building (above) FMSR stands for Federated Malay States Railway. Completed in 1909, the building is possibly the world's grandest railway station without trains. From 1903, it was possible to travel from Butterworth to Kuala Lumpur by rail. Passengers purchased an all-inclusive rail ticket from Penang for a journey that started in a waiting room, continued by railway ferry steamer to Butterworth, and finally was completed by train through the Peninsula. The Royal Malaysian Customs Department now occupies the building.

The Oversea-Chinese Banking Corporation (OCBC) of Singapore opened a branch office on Beach Street in 1920. Global economic problems took their toll on early forms of the bank but a beautiful Art Deco-styled building was constructed in 1934. While no longer occupied by the bank, the original bank logo can be seen on the front façade.

Heritage Restoration

Penang's trade and wealth are reflected in its mansions and monumental commercial and eclectic buildings of the late Victorian era. Many are ornately decorated with colourful tiles and elaborately carved Chinese doors. While George Town's UNESCO status restricts certain development, it encourages restoration and reuse with many places offering creative and innovative spaces within their heritage façade. Old shoplots and houses have picked up on the tourism boom and now sell a variety of items and services such as flavoured shaved ice, coffee, souvenirs, drinks and bicycle hire. Boutique heritage accommodation and cafés are now a hallmark of George Town.

Left and opposite: Armenian Street (Lebuh Armenian) is one of the liveliest heritage streets offering a mix of old houses, shoplots, refurbished cafés, boutique hotels, museums and shops. The street was formerly known as Malay Lane because of a Malay kampung that was once on this site. The original Chinese name was Pak Thang-Ah Kay or Copper Worker's Street as copper and brass were once made and traded here. Armenian traders, being mostly Christians, established their churches here but interestingly, there appears to be no evidence today of Armenian activity in the street now named after them.

Left: Gerakbudaya, a small independent bookshop in a refitted shophouse on Jalan Masjid Kapitan Keling (the former Pitt Street), in the heart of the heritage zone.

Right: Cheong Fatt Tze (14 Leith St) or the Blue Mansion is considered by Lonely Planet as one of the world's ten best mansions. What is now a boutique hotel was once the home of a wealthy Chinese tycoon, Cheong Fatt Tze. Constructed in the late 19th century, it is a traditional but ornate two-storey, Chinese courtyard house built in Hakka-Teochew style incorporating feng shui principles. This stately home has won many heritage awards and featured in several movies. Visitors can stay here or take one of three daily guided tours.

Below: ChinaHouse (153 Beach St) in George Town is an excellent example of heritage refurbishment. This property extends over three former shoplots and is now a multipurpose restaurant, café, bar, art gallery and retail outlet. Coffee Junkie @ Junk (401 Chulia St) retains much of its original charm as a tiny junk shop with the addition of seating and premium coffee blends.

Below: Muntri Suites,
23 Love Lane, Macalister Mansion, Clove Hall
(pictured), Eight Rooms and Seven Terraces also
offer boutique heritage accommodation.

Above and top: The Edison on Leith Street was built in 1906 as a
family house for a wealthy Chinese trader along a street known as
'Millionaire's Row'. From the 1960s until 2012, it was the Cathay
Hotel, popular with backpackers. Now renovated, this heritage
boutique property of 35 rooms appeals to those seeking uniquely
deluxe Penang accommodation.

Clan Houses and Museums

Clan houses are another unique feature of historic George Town. These communal organizations evolved to offer recently arrived Chinese immigrants shelter and support in their formative years in Penang. Clan associations of dialect groups known as *kongsi* created an elaborate infrastructure that included houses and temples and in some cases, they were also the base for secret societies. Cantonese and Hokkien immigrants with names such as Tan, Yeoh, Yap, Khoo, Cheah and Lim became part of Penang's *kongsi* communities.

Right: The Yap Kongsi (71 Armenian St) is a Straits Eclectic style building erected in 1924 after two Yap families merged. Adjoining it is a temple which was restored in 1998 as a place where the descendants of the Hokkien Yaps could come to pray. It has an ornate gable decoration featuring a dragon made from intricate porcelain shard work called 'chien nien'.

Left: Cannon Square is home to the grandest kongsi, Khoo Kongsi (with three entrances but the main one on Cannon St), which looked after the welfare of the Hokkien clan. The Khoos were already well established in Melaka before the pioneer family members arrived in Penang in 1835. Over time, they created a mini clan village offering a strong social welfare function. There is an ornate temple here, and Chinese opera plus the occasional concert are performed in the square. On the last weekend of each month, Khoo Kongsi features a light display. Khoo Kongsi has been restored but retains its historic, semi-feudal and defensive setting. This includes a temple, traditional theatre, association building and terrace houses around an expansive square. Its temple was constructed in 1906 by artisans from China replacing a temple which had previously burnt down. Ancestral tablets are housed in the temple which has an ornate carved and gilded entrance.

Left: George Town has several interesting museums including Pinang Peranakan Mansion (20 Church St) which is a delightfully restored mansion that celebrates the contribution of the Nonyas and Babas to Penang life. Antiques, jewellery and opulent furniture and interiors are featured. Wealthy Peranakans lead a gracious life surrounded by the grandeur of imported materials, such as Scottish ironwork balustrades.

Below left: No 120 Armenian St was a hotbed of Chinese revolutionary politics from 1910 to 1911. This terrace house was the Southeast Asian base for the nationalist revolutionary organization known as Tung Meng Hooi. Chinese national Dr. Sun Yat Sen (known as the 'father of modern China') resided here and planned the Canton March, an important event in the Chinese Revolution that led to the overthrow of the Ching Dynasty. The building is now a museum and well worth visiting.

Below right: The Penang Islamic Museum (128 Armenian St) is located in the former home of Syed Alatas. This Straits Eclectic-style home built in 1860 has been restored and is now a museum portraying the development of Islam in Penang. It is one of few buildings along the street with Islamic architectural references.

Places of Worship

George Town's many places of worship reflect the harmonious relations between the people of many different races, creeds and religions who now live in Penang.

Below: *Acheen Street Mosque (on Lebuh Acheh) with its Arab-style minaret was built in 1808 as one of Penang's first mosques. The surrounding district was home to Penang's first Arab traders and the mosque was donated by an Aceh-Arabian.*

Right: *Nearby, the larger Kapitan Kling Mosque founded in 1801, features distinctive domes. It was established to give the Muslim division of troops from the East India Company a place of worship. The temple is named after the Muslim community's headman who also became its first superintendent. It has seen several additions over the years.*

Right: A Catholic bishop arrived in Penang not long after the British settlement was established. The current Church of the Assumption isn't the original structure as it only dates to 1861. In 1955 the church was designated a cathedral by a Vatican decree but reverted to a church in 2003 when parishioner numbers dwindled.

Below: The Tua Pek Kong Temple and adjoining buildings at the corner of King and Gereja Streets offer a striking architectural façade. This Taoist temple is dedicated to Zhang Li, a Chinese immigrant who landed in Penang in the mid 18th century well before British settlement. The locals began to worship him as Tua Pek Kong, who is the "great uncle" and god of prosperity.

The Waterfront

George Town's main waterfront area extends from the Eastern and Oriental Hotel (the E & O) beyond the *padang* (open field), Fort Cornwallis and Swettenham Pier to various clan jetties. Many visitors arrive from the mainland via the car and passenger ferry terminal at Pengkalan Weld. At the turn of the 20th century, the railway line from Butterworth to Taiping was completed and was well on the way to Kuala Lumpur. Penang's port facilities needed upgrading to cope with the export of tin and other goods. The coastline was reclaimed and a 183-m (600-ft) long pier was completed in 1904. It was named Swettenham Pier after the Resident General of the Federated Malay States, Sir Frank Swettenham. By 1911, the pier had been extended to 366 m (1,200 ft) and business boomed. While cargo is now mostly handled in Butterworth and most travellers fly into Penang, the new Swettenham Pier is an important berth for cruise ships.

Opposite below: While development in the historic downtown UNESCO zone is restricted, in other parts, the sky is the limit for hotels and condominiums that strive to maximize their sea views.

Above: George Town's various Chinese clans established their own jetties to service the boats in the harbour. The Hokkien clan jetties along Weld Quay became dwellings in the late 19th century and are still used by members of the Ong, Lim, Chew Tan, Lee and Yeoh families. Simple shelters were built on the jetties which serviced ships moored in the harbour. Built on stilts over the water, what are now houses are well established but visitors are welcome to stroll around.

Above: To get a bird's eye view of Penang, visit the Rainbow Skywalk, the highest outdoor glass sky walk in Malaysia. It's located at the top of Komtar, the tallest skyscraper in George Town.

Left: Penang's Eastern and Oriental Hotel (E & O) is Malaysia's only truly grand hotel. Opened by the Sarkies Brothers from Armenia, the E & O along with their other properties, Raffles (Singapore) and The Strand (Yangon) were the hotels of choice amongst discerning and well-heeled travellers. Once billed as the finest hotel east of the Suez, the E & O, built in 1885, has seen various restorations, refurbishments and expansions including the new Victory Annexe and is now very different from the original. Its old and original wing is the most historically authentic in which each suite is furnished with period furniture and spacious bathrooms. Its 1885 Restaurant is the venue for traditional afternoon teas plus elegant and refined dining. Guests can stroll along the seaside promenade and enjoy cocktails in Farquhar's Bar overlooking the pool.

Street Art

This page: Street art has revitalized George Town; some of this seems by design some by default. A conscious effort to inject some fun and interactive art into the urbanscape is apparent. Much of what is on offer is the work of Lithuanian artist Ernest Zacharevic whose creativity has the tourists lining to be photographed with artwork such as the "bicycle children".

Zacharevic has often been referred to as the Malaysian-based Banksy; the pseudonym for the famous UK-based graffiti artist. Both address often controversial topics and use physical props to add realism to their art.

This page: Other Penang street art installations were commissioned by the authorities and Kuala Lumpur companies. Sculpture at Work answered the call of the "Marking of George Town Project" with 52 specially designed steel rod caricatures. These installations provide valuable historic information in a more lively fashion than traditional historic markers.

Chapter 3: Around George Town

Air Itam

A number of British pioneers such as James Scott and David Brown successfully established large agricultural estates and grew pepper, nutmeg, cloves and cinnamon. The Far East India Company had a 53-ha (130-acre) spice garden in Air Itam, a township just 6 km (3½ miles) from George Town.

This page: Penang's scenic and historic funicular railway dating back to 1923 operates from Air Itam (sometimes spelt as Ayer Itam or Ayer Hitam) to the summit of Penang Hill (now officially called Bukit Bendera but to most locals, it's still known as Penang Hill).

Colonialists used to travel to the summit of Penang Hill above Air Itam in sedan chairs carried by "coolies" or by pony and trap. This changed on October 21, 1923 with the opening of the Penang Hill Railway (an earlier attempt to construct a railway failed). Work on the funicular railway (two trains connected to each other via cables act as a counterbalance to each other) commenced in 1906 and was completed 17 years later. Starting from Air Itam, the 2,007-m (2,195-yard) ascent now takes just 11 minutes to the summit at Flagstaff Hill with regular daily departures from 6.30 am until 9 pm. There are several intermediate stations for the locals to alight and the railway passes terraced slopes and old colonial homesteads. The blue, air-conditioned, Swiss-made coaches accommodate 100 passengers.

Above: Kek Lok Si Buddhist Temple (this translates from Hokkien as the Temple of Supreme Bliss) built on the side of Penang Hill dominates the Air Itam skyline. The seven-storey high main pagoda is also known as the Pagoda of 10,000 Buddhas. It is reputedly Southeast Asia's largest Buddhist temple. Construction commenced in 1890 and appears to be ongoing as new structures are forever being added. It is a steep ascent from the base to the highest point and can be crowded especially at Chinese New Year. The temple incorporates elements of Chinese, Thai and Burmese architecture in its elaborate design.

Penang Hill

Penang Hill, including several other hills such as Flagstaff Hill, was identified and settled by 1810. As such, it was the region's first hill station predating those in India and other parts of the region. Colonialists sought refuge from the heat and humidity of the lowlands. The lowlands were also a breeding ground of disease with inefficient sanitation and Penang Hill offered a cleaner and healthier environment. Despite the two-hour pony ride to the top, the recuperative air was worth the journey.

Higher slopes were reserved for high ranking civil servants with the Governor's residence at Flagstaff Hill. In 1865, writer John Cameron noted that the hill was dotted with neatly built bungalows "where a climate is obtained differing but little from a mild summer in Europe". Reproducing life back home was important including planting temperate fruits such as strawberries.

Above: Visitors can stay in the colonial surroundings of the Hotel Bellevue Penang Hill. David Brown's Restaurant and Tea Terraces at Strawberry Hill offer good views and relaxed dining.

Below: Views from the summit top at 830 m (2,723 feet) near the Hotel Bellevue vary according to the air quality but on clear days, those towards George Town and across to Butterworth are good.

Opposite: Sri Aruloli Thirumurugan Temple is an elaborately decorated Hindu temple also offering good views.

Penang Botanic Gardens

Penang Botanic Gardens are another colonial initiative opened by the British in 1884 as the Waterfall Gardens. Now an important green lung for the island, the gardens are open from 5am to 8pm and are used for recreation, exercise and education.

Above: Facilities include parking, picnic areas, refreshments and souvenirs. The gardens are 8 km (5 miles) from George Town and are accessible via public bus. There is a 5-km (3-mile), sealed jeep track from the quarry near the entrance of the garden to Penang Hill. This is to provide access for hill residents but is also popular with mountain bikers and hikers.

Top: One of the most fascinating plants in the Botanic Gardens is the Cannon Ball Tree (Couroupita guianensis) with its large, woody and spherical brown fruits that measure up to 25 cm (10 in) in width and grow from the trunk. This deciduous tree is related to the Brazil nut and is a native of South and Central America.

This page: The 29-ha (72-acre) gardens are located in an old granite quarry and are surrounded by forests and dissected by several streams. The main aims of the gardens are to support conservation, recreation and research. There is a Garden Shop and pre-arranged guided tours are available for groups.

Chapter 4: North Coast

There are three main beaches along the northern coastal strip – starting from the east is Tanjung Bungah, then Batu Ferringhi and the more tranquil fishing village of Teluk Bahang to the west.

Tanjung Bungah

While there are some hotels and resorts located along Tanjung Bungah at the eastern extremity of the Batu Ferringhi stretch, the seaside district is increasingly becoming home to luxurious sea-facing condominiums. One of the world's largest collections of dolls, toys and models is housed in the Penang Toy Museum Heritage Garden located in Tanjung Bungah. Malaysia's first floating mosque is situated by the sea here (see page 14).

Left: The narrow coastal strip along Penang's north coast is lined with medium- to high-rise condominiums. From Tanjung Tokong on the island's far north-east, the beaches extend westward with Tanjung Bungah (foreground) being a mixed area of hotels, condominiums and seaside houses.

Opposite below: Tanjung Bungah is not as popular with tourists as the main Batu Ferringhi beachfront. However, developers have constructed new high-rise condominiums along the beachfront to cater to a growing demand from affluent locals and an increasing number of foreign investors who are attracted by the climate and seaside location.

Batu Ferringhi

The palm and casuarina-lined northern beachfront of Batu Ferringhi (Foreigner's Rock) caters to mostly foreign tourists in being home to deluxe resorts, cafés, bars, restaurants, small shops and the ever-popular night bazaar.

The Batu Ferringhi Night Market opens each evening at about 5pm and lasts until midnight. It stretches for most of the way along the main road of Jalan Batu Ferringhi and is mostly patronized by the tourists staying in the resorts along the beach.

Many outlets sprawl along either side of the road to offer a mesmerizing selection of resort clothing, sunglasses, DVDs, beachwear, beachside sporting accessories and souvenirs. Haggling adds to the experience and enjoyment of this lively market. Interspersed amongst the retail mayhem are bars, restaurants and cafés offering local cuisines as well as many others from around the globe.

Established international hotel brands such as PARKROYAL Penang, Shangri-La, Hard Rock, Holiday Inn Resort, Four Points by Sheraton, Copthorne Orchid, Double Tree Resort by Hilton sit side by side with local brands such as Bayview Beach, Lone Pine and Hotel Naza Talyya.

The waters off Batu Ferringhi are mostly calm and the long stretches of gently sloping golden sands make them ideal for family fun in the sun.

Below: The PARKROYAL Penang is typical of most of the resorts along the strip in being a well-established property offering deluxe sea-view accommodation and a location immediately on the Batu Ferringhi sands set amongst lush tropical gardens. The PARKROYAL Resort offers a comprehensive range of leisure activities, restaurants, bars, children's club and spa.

Above and top: The Lone Pine Hotel was the first hotel to be located along Batu Ferringhi when a colonial mansion situated here was converted in 1948 to a small hotel of just ten rooms. It still retains its colonial elements although contemporary design and functionality were incorporated during various renovations. Whistling casuarina trees provide a special charm that has always appealed to tourists.

Left: Watersport activities along the northern beaches are offered by both the resorts here and private operators. Sections of the beach are reserved for motorized watersports such as jet skis and parasailing while the rest of the beach is for passive sports such as kayaking and Top Cat catamaran sailing.

Above: The afternoons are special times on Batu Ferringhi beach as many of the hotel residents take to the beaches in the cooler part of the day. The winds and weather conditions are ideal in the afternoon for adventurous visitors to be launched high in the sky for an exhilarating parasail over the sea.

Right: In the late afternoon, the bars and restaurants along Batu Ferringhi open for thirsty and hungry guests, who arrive to take in the sun setting over Penang National Park on the far north-west of the island.

Left: Spas such as St. Gregory's in the PARKROYAL Penang offer an extensive menu of massages, facials and therapeutic treatments in the luxurious spa or massages in an open-sided pavilion in the resort garden.

Below left: At other times of the day, guests are happy to laze around the pool beneath shaded coconut palms, figs and casuarina trees. The larger resorts along the beach strip provide a comprehensive range of activities on both land and sea.

Below: Many outlets such as Uncle Zack by the Beach in the PARKROYAL Penang are open to the elements and are cooled by refreshing sea breezes. Local and international dishes are offered plus an enticing selection of cool beverages including wines from around the world.

Teluk Bahang

The road from Batu Ferringhi weaves its way beside the coastline to a small Malay fishing village at Teluk Bahang. While a large resort once operated here and its future remains uncertain, the shaded tree-line beach is pleasant for swimming. The road ends at the village and turns southward down the island's west coast. Penang National Park (this part of the national park was formerly known as Pantai Aceh Forest Reserve) lies immediately behind Teluk Bahang and boats can be chartered here for the journey into the remote and beautiful Monkey Beach within the park.

Opposite: The Tropical Spice Garden at Teluk Bahang is a 3.2-ha (8-acre) forested area that is home to over 500 species of tropical flora. Well formed trails throughout provide ease of access but maintain the ambiance of a natural area. There are special plant collections of bamboos, ferns, orchids, gingers and rare palms. Visitors can learn about the history of the spice trade regionally and of Penang from the audio tour stop at Spice Globe.

With so many native rainforest trees in the garden, it isn't surprising that animals make there home here too. Observant visitors may see monkeys, squirrels and reptiles.

The garden is open daily during daylight hours and visitors enjoy a complimentary guided tour of the Spice Terraces to see Asia's most popular spices and herbs. Herbal tea is served in the Bamboo Garden.

Above: Big leaves and large flowers ensure that the Bat Lily (Tacca integrifolia) is a popular ornamental flower. This purple and white flower is a native of the region as well as of tropical Africa and Australia. Visitors to the Tropical Spice Garden can see this and many other colourful flowers.

Left: Some of the interesting flowers growing here include the Sexy Pink Heliconia (Heliconia chartacea). Heliconia species are native to the rainforests of South America especially Brazil and Guyana. They are related to the banana and display colourful pendulous flowering stems. Unlike other Heliconia, this cultivar has distinctive pink flower bracts.

Chapter 5: West Coast

Penang's west coast extends from Penang National Park southwards through small villages, farms, forested areas and mangroves lining the coastline along the Straits of Malacca. Within a short distance from the busy Batu Ferringhi strip, the mountainous landscape is dominated by forests and farms. The few people still employed in Penang's agricultural sector work in farms and plantations located on the west coast. Crops grown include rice, fruits, rubber, oil palm, vegetables and spices. Mechanization is now a feature of rice production which is centred on villages such as Sungai Burung.

Right: Kampung Sungai Pinang is a typical village on the west coast where traditional and modern housing can be seen.

Below right: Many people on the west coast still live in villages called 'kampungs'. While houses in these villages are mostly made from modern building materials these days, it's not unusual to see traditional timber houses. Some of these are old while others are modern but built along traditional lines. They stand on stilts to enable cooling from circulating air. Overhanging eaves and shuttered windows in very old houses were adopted as additional cooling methods. While most houses now have metal or tiled roofs, traditional houses had attap (woven palm leaves). An exterior staircase often covered in ornately decorated tiles leads to a large porch where guests are entertained before entering the privacy of the house proper.

Left: Well formed trails provide access to the key sites and the variety of habitats supported in the park. Seeking the assistance of a professional guide is recommended as much of the forest detail is camouflaged and at a macro level, so not seen by many who pass through.

Above: Waterfalls like Titi Kerawang situated close to the main road provide a cool location in which to bathe or take a photograph. The pink granite rock provides a photogenic backdrop and fruit stalls near the entrance, a refreshing break.

Left: Teluk Bahang Dam is located on the island's north-western side and each year in June, Penang's famous dragon boat races are contested here (see page 34).

West Coast Attractions

Two of the west coast's most popular and educational attractions are the Entopia by Penang Butterfly Farm and Tropical Fruit Farm just a few kilometres out of Teluk Bahang.

These pages: Entopia by Penang Butterfly Farm is a living butterfly and insect exhibition with thousands of colourful creatures flitting around the large enclosed gardens that contain hundreds of nectar plants. Visitors can expect to see over 50 Malaysian butterfly species at any one time.

Chapter 6: South by South-east

All visitors who arrive in Penang by air will land at Penang International Airport at Bayan Lepas in the south-east of the island. Many industries are grouped around the airport which is a strategic hub for receiving and dispatching goods. Much of the industry is located within a Free Trade Zone centred on Bayan Lepas (Malaysia's Silicon Valley). The main industries are electronics and manufacturing operated by some of the world's largest companies. Some 43% of Penang's working population is employed in manufacturing.

Right top: The Snake Temple at Sungai Kluang near Bayan Lepas on the way to the airport is a popular tourist stop because of its resident snakes found curled around the altar. These snakes are Wagler's Pit Vipers (also appropriately known as Temple Pit Vipers or Tropidolaemus wagleri) and are quite common in the forests of Southeast Asia. This Buddhist temple dates back to 1850 and is dedicated to Choo Sor Kong, a Buddhist monk known to have provided shelter to reptiles. While venomous, the viper isn't considered aggressive and those in the temple have been de-venomed. The snakes also live in the trees at the side of the temple and there is an adjoining Snake Farm where other species are housed.

Right below: Queensbay Mall, in Bayan Lepas, is Penang's largest shopping centre. It offers a comprehensive range of retail outlets from department stores to boutiques, restaurants, banks and entertainment outlets including a skating rink and cinemas. It also serves as a terminal for buses from Kuala Lumpur.

Above: Penang is connected to the mainland by two of the region's longest bridges. The first bridge was opened in 1985 and is 13.5 km (8 $\frac{1}{2}$ miles) long, while the second (pictured) opened in early 2014. This second crossing is a dual-carriageway toll bridge, 24 km (15 miles) long, that crosses from Batu Kawan on the mainland to Batu Maung on the island. It is now Malaysia's longest bridge and the second longest in Southeast Asia. Passenger and car ferries still ply the channel from George Town to Butterworth.

Right: The Penang War Museum (Bukit Batu Bayan near Bayan Lepas) was built by the British in the 1930s. It was meant to protect Penang from sea invasion but on 17 December, 1941 the Japanese attacked and successfully overran the fort with a land-based invasion. The 8-ha (20-acre) site is now Southeast Asia's largest war museum and is open for visitors to see old cannons, buildings, gun emplacements and other artefacts.

Beaches

While the beaches of the south-east and south are not as inviting as those along Batu Ferringhi, they do have their own charm. The shallow waters attract local families who come to relax away from the crowds at the more popular beaches. Shaded, tree-lined beaches provide a tranquil setting and a place to escape the heat. Several fishing communities live along the coast, mooring their small wooden boats along creeks that flow into the sea.

Above: *Teluk Kumbar located between Bayan Lepas and Balik Pulau is a peaceful beach popular with the locals but rarely sought out by visitors. Those who venture down this far will discover a relaxed setting with few other people along the sandy foreshore.*

Top: *Batu Maung on Penang's south-eastern tip is one such fishing community where a giant footprint on a boulder has generated various myths and legends. The area is also well known with Penangites who come to large beachside restaurants such as Hai Boey for fresh seafood dishes.*

Left: While most tourists stay in George Town or Batu Ferringhi, the proximity of the south-east to the airport and the industries around Bayan Lepas, makes hotels such as the Hotel Equatorial Penang a viable proposition. This 662-room property is perched 107 m (250 ft) above sea level and offers commanding views of the adjoining and picturesque, 18-hole, championship Penang Golf Club as well as of George Town in the distance. The Hotel Equatorial has numerous features including a landscaped outdoor pool with waterfalls and natural jacuzzis.

Islands

There are several small islands off the coast of the main island only two of which have settlements of any substance. Jerejak Island is home to a rainforest resort and Aman Island has a fishing village. Over the decades, Jerejak has been a leper colony, quarantine station and penal colony. It was also considered as a suitable location for a military fort but this didn't proceed. Jerejak became a processing centre for new migrants to Penang and then a sanatorium for tuberculosis patients. From 1969 to 1993 it was a maximum security prison, and was nicknamed the Alcatraz of Malaysia. Aman Island contains a small fishing village and is just 15 minutes from the mainland jetty. Fishing and jungle trekking are popular activities and various floating restaurants make it a place for the locals to dine on seafood. Also just off the coast are Rimau Island and Betong Island with the latter having homestay accommodation.

Above and left: Jerejak Resort offers accommodation and adventure sports, such as abseiling, rock climbing, mountain biking and jungle trekking, as well as fishing.

Opposite page: Located off the south-eastern coastline of the main island, Jerejak Island is the largest island at 363 ha (895 acres) and is just a short ferry journey from the terminal at Bayan Lepas on Penang Island. Jerejak Rainforest Resort and Spa now operates here.

Chapter 7: Butterworth

Visitors to Penang Island may want to venture across the Straits of Malacca to the port of Butterworth on the mainland. The passenger and vehicular ferry still provides an important link from George Town to the mainland.

Right: While not particularly scenic, the ferry ride to Butterworth is interesting and the sea breezes refreshing. Butterworth's shoreline is dominated by wharves where many goods for the island and the north are unloaded.

Above: The fast Electric Train Service (ETS) operates return services from Kuala Lumpur to Butterworth. From here, passengers can walk to the passenger/car ferry that connects to Penang Island. Express trains depart from Kuala Lumpur's Sentral Station and stop at a few major stations along the four-hour journey, the main stops on the Penang mainland being Bukit Mertajam and Butterworth. Services are popular and tickets can be purchased in advance online. There is a small snack bar serving drinks and light meals. Trains also head north from Butterworth to Padang Besar on the Thai border with connections from there on Thai trains to Hat Yai and beyond.

Opposite: Sree Maha Mariamman Devasthanam Temple in Butterworth is an ornately decorated Hindu temple dedicated to the mother deity, Amman. While the original temple was built in 1853, the current colourful temple only dates back to 1980. It is Butterworth's biggest and oldest Hindu temple and features an ornate 'gopuram' or entrance gate.

Getting About

Penang International Airport is serviced by local airlines Malaysia Airlines, AirAsia and Firefly which operate both domestic and international flights from this northern Malaysian hub, as well as Malindo Air, a domestic carrier. Other international airlines provide services to destinations in neighbouring Indonesia, Thailand, Singapore, China and Taiwan.

There are high speed ferries operating between Penang and Medan on the neighbouring Indonesian island of Sumatra. Cruise ships use the terminal facilities at Port Swettenham along the George Town waterfront.

In addition to the two toll bridges across to the mainland, passenger and car ferries still ply the channel from George Town to Butterworth. The departure point on the island is from the jetty located along the waterfront within the heritage zone. On the mainland, the North-South Expressway, stretching from the Thai border down to Singapore, provides access to the Peninsula.

Trains operate from the terminal in Butterworth. From here it is possible to catch trains to the north of Malaysia and on to Thailand and southwards to Kuala Lumpur and on to Singapore.

Trishaws are still a common form of transport in the city centre. Some trishaw riders basically use their bicycle as a home and transport the locals to and from the markets while others are ornately decorated to cater to tourists. Other tourists choose to hire a bicycle and cycle around George Town's historic locations.

Left: Trishaws provide a slow and leisurely way of travelling around George Town.

Above: A funicular railway ride to the summit of Penang Hill is one of the 'must do' activities.

Opposite: Car and passenger ferries connect Penang Island to the mainland.

Resources

Contacts

ChinaHouse Penang: www.chinahouse.com.my

Entopia by Penang Butterfly Farm: www.entopia.com

ESCAPE Adventureplay: www.escape.my

Freedom Getaway Adventures: www.freedomgetaway.org

FTZ Travel and Tours: www.ftz.com.my

George Town Festival: www.georgetownfestival.com

GLOW Penang by Zinc: www.glowbyzinc.com/penang

PARKROYAL Penang Resort: www.parkroyalhotels.com

Penang Botanic Gardens: botanicalgardens.penang.gov.my

Penang Global Tourism: www.mypenang.gov.my

Penang Island Jazz Festival: www.penangjazz.com

Pinang Peranakan Mansion:
    www.pinangperanakanmansion.com.my

The Edison: www.theedisonhotels.com

The Habitat Penang Hill: thehabitat.my

Tropical Fruit Farm: www.tropicalfruitfarm.com.my

Tropical Spice Garden: tropicalspicegarden.com

References

Barber, A. *Penang under the East India Company 1786-1858*. Malaysia.

Bird, Isabella L. 2011 (first published 1883). *The Golden Chersonese and the Way Thither*. John Beaufoy Publishing.

Bowden, D. 2012. *Enchanting Malaysia*. John Beaufoy Publishing.

Bowden, D., Hicks N. and Shippen M. 2013. *Southeast Asia: A Region Revealed*. John Beaufoy Publishing.

Films

Penang is a movie set just waiting to be noticed by location scouts. Movies such as *Anna and the King*, *The Touch* and *Indochine* (1992 Oscar for Best Foreign Language Film) were filmed in Penang.

Acknowledgements

Many people are involved in producing a book of this scope. The author acknowledges the support provided by Narelle McMurtrie and Alison Fraser (ChinaHouse), Francois Sigrist (Parkroyal Penang Resort), Silvan Neuteboom (GLOW Penang by Zinc), Joseph Teoh (Freedom Getaway Adventures), Geok Ling, Pauline Yoon and Darren Ng (Penang Global Tourism), FTZ Travel and Tours, Andrew Barber for invaluable input to Penang's history and Erik Fearn (www.skypix.com.my) for the stunning aerial photographs.

The publishers and the author would like to express special thanks to Ken Scriven (1928–2018) for his advice and support during the preparation of this book.

About the Author

David Bowden is a freelance photojournalist based in Malaysia who specializes in travel and the environment. While Australian, he's been in Asia for longer than he can remember and returns to his home country as a tourist. When he's not travelling the world, he enjoys relaxing with his equally adventurous wife Maria and daughter Zoe. He is also the author of other books in the Enchanting series on Borneo, Singapore, Malaysia, Vietnam, Bali & Lombok and Langkawi.

Index

This edition published in the United Kingdom in 2019 by John Beaufoy Publishing,
11 Blenheim Court, 316 Woodstock Road, Oxford OX2 7NS, England
www.johnbeaufoy.com

ISBN 978-1-912081-83-7

Original design by Glyn Bridgewater
Cover design by Ginny Zeal
Cartography by William Smuts
Project management by Rosemary Wilkinson

Printed and bound in Malaysia by Times Offset (M) Sdn. Bhd.

All photos by David Bowden except:
George Town Festival (p.33 left); Izlyn Syahnaz (p.39 bottom); Komtar (p.36 bottom); Entopia by Penang Butterfly
Farm (p.66, top); Penang Global Tourism (p.2, p.16 right); Skypix (p.6 bottom left); The Habitat (p.35, bottom).

Cover captions and credits
Back cover (left to right): *Entrance to Peranakan House* © David Bowden; *Ornate roof of Yap Temple, Armenian
Street* © David Bowden; *Rickshaw outside fire station* © David Bowden; *Penang Butterfly Farm* © David Bowden.
Front cover top (left to right): *The Habitat Penang Hill* © The Habitat; *Grey Pansy butterfly* © David Bowden; *Street
art, Armenian Street* © David Bowden; *Eastern & Oriental Hotel* © David Bowden.
Front cover (main image): *Cheong Fatt Tze (Blue) Mansion, Georgetown* © Shutterstock/Toni Schmidt.